AF381743

Éditions DIASPORAS NOIRES

www.diasporas-noires.com

©Emmanuel Ngombet 2019
ISBN digital version : 9782490931040
ISBN printed version : 9782490931057
Date of digital publication : February 2020

Emmanuel NGOMBET OTSARO DITUNGA

THE UNITED STATES OF WEST AFRICA - USOWA

Essay

Collection Savoirs

Traduction du français à l'anglais : Joséphine Ndiaye

SUMMARY

Foreword...9

1. Creation of the United States of West Africa.................. 11

2. Constitution of the USOWA (USWA)..........................12

PREAMBLE 12

ARTICLE ONE 12

ARTICLE II...22

ARTICLE III..24

ARTICLE IV...26

ARTICLE V...28

ARTICLE VI...28

ARTICLE VII 29

SUGGESTED AMENDMENTS 30

ARTICLE I 30

ARTICLE II...30

ARTICLE III..30

ARTICLE IV... 31

ARTICLE V... 31

ARTICLE VI... 31

ARTICLE VII 32

ARTICLE VIII 32

ARTICLE IX 32

ARTICLE X...33

ARTICLE XI 33

ARTICLE XII 33

ARTICLE XIII 35

ARTICLE XIV 35

ARTICLE XV 36

ARTICLE XVI 37

ARTICLE XVII 37

ARTICLE XVIII 38

ARTICLE XIX 38

ARTICLE XX 39

ARTICLE XXI 40

ARTICLE XXII 40

ARTICLE XXIII 42

ARTICLE XXIV 42

3. The starry golden spiral, the flag, and its meaning. 43

4. This partially united Africa motto 45

5. The anthem of the Light carriers 47

6. PanAfrican emergencies 59

Anticipation 60

Anticipation 1 : Symbolic creation of : USOWA (USWA)   60

Anticipation 2 : Creation of African gold reserves 61

Anticipation 3. Dissemination of Knowledge in African languages   62

Anticipation 4 and 5. Fresh water and arable Lands resources 63

Anticipation 6 64

Anticipation 7 64

7. Backbone and foundations of the federal state 67

7.1. Detailed explanations about the Africa gold reserves 69

I. CREATION OF THE GOLD RESERVES OFFICE OF DEPOSITS AND CONSIGNATIONS (AGRODC) 69

6

II. OBJECTIVES 69

III. Panafrican federative cash operations 70

7.2 Just a word on the single currency of the federal state 71

7.3. The search engine with African content 72

8. Action taken to build the desirable future for Humanity . 73

Appendix 75

Press Release 75

The Kaolack Gas Terminal Project in Senegal at Kaolack ... 83

University poles project for West Africa.............................. 84

UNITED STATES OF WEST AFRICA – USOWA 86

MANIFESTATION OF INTEREST.....................................86

Dedication 93

Bibliography 95

From the same author 97

Foreword

Perhaps quite unwittingly, and indeed despite his own will, Alassane Dramane OUATTARA, by making his proposal for the ECO-Euro parity, ECO being the new single currency for ECOWAS countries; has just declared the end of micro-states, such as defined when they first became independent.

Will the ECO become the new name of the CFA franc? Yes, at least in the first instance, as the west african single currency will be issued at a fixed rate with respect to the euro, Alassane Ouattara explained. « To this day, the exchange rate euro/cfa franc is, 655,9.

And of course, would the heads of state decide next year to change the CFA franc into ECO because we would have fully respected the exchange rate convergence criterion, this rate would remain the same in the immediate future. »
He would not hear the protest of Italy or Germany appalled that the cfa franc system be still going on, allowing The French government to legally pluck up to 400 billions euros from African countries by using the cfa franc every year. The point is -whether he ignores it or not- while making that statement-, that times have changed. The African youth resents this sort of extension of the cfa franc system throughout western African countries, and they feel as if that this situation will become an extension of the French empire colonial slavery, -and even worse-, of Europe upon Africa.

Proponents say that the use of a single currency will facilitate Trade, reduce banking transaction costs and facilitate payments.

Among the 385 millions people living in the ECOWAS space.

On the other hand, critics fear Nigeria domination on the monetary policy, due to its greater economic strength in the area; which would delay the direct economic benefits for the others.
"No developing country – West African countries included, is immune to monetary shocks caused by policies implemented by other countries.
Our Heads of States stay contented with the single
Currency system (euro/eco), or even to the sterling pound, dollar, or the Yuan (just to highlight obsession over that single currency system). The single currency system is seen as a tool for keeping inflation on target, without allowing any growth, which is critical to support development.

While now being free, the former slaves, instead of leaving the comfortable farms of their old masters, would rather stay there and receive a salary as an abundant work force.
Today Black slaveholders are working hard to bring those enriched freed men to a voluntary submission to the master's authority.

Do the young Africans have to submit to these new forms of slavery that have been taking away the autonomy of Black people for six centuries ?

1. Creation of the United States of West Africa

The citizens and civil society will be the incentive for the implementation of a West African federal state throughout Africa. African people must now move from complaints to challenge, then from action to anticipation.

In May 2020, the west African civil society is going to officially proceed to the symbolic creation of the USOWA/USWA, in Ghana, Burkina Faso and even Benin.

The federal state (USWA) will overrule the talk over all the micro-states convergence criteria, for the single currency constitutes the "backbone and foundation" which is essential to the existence of this African nation.

Are we able to anticipate our common future ?

Initialize raising funds from public and private owners (the citizen is a shareholder then becomes an actor) for the constitution of gold and currency reserves, necessary to West African countries for the creation of a single currency :
The ECOWAS WARI-WARA.

2. Constitution of the USOWA (USWA)

CONSTITUTION OF THE UNITED STATES OF WEST
AFRICA

PREAMBLE

We, People of the 15 countries of the current West Africa States (Benin, Burkina Faso, Cape-Verde, Ivory Coast, the Gambia, Ghana, Bissau-Guinea, Guinea Conakry, Liberia, Mali, Niger, Nigeria, Senegal, Sierra Leone, Togo), in order to form a more perfect Union, establish Justice, insure domestic Tranquility, provide for the common defence, promote the general Welfare, and secure the Blessings of Liberty to ourselves and our Posterity, do ordain and establish this Constitution for the United States of West Africa.

ARTICLE ONE

Section 1.
All legislative Powers herein granted shall be vested in a Congress of The United States of West Africa which shall consist of a Senate And a House of Representatives.

Section 2.

The House of Representatives shall be composed of members chosen every third year by the people of the several States and the Electors in each State shall have the qualification requisite for Electors of the most numerous Branch of the State Legislature.

No Person shall be a Representative who shall not have attained the age of twenty five years, and been seven years a Citizen, of the United States of West Africa, and who shall not, when elected, be a inhabitant of that State in which he shall be chosen.

Representatives and direct taxes shall be apportioned among the different states which may be included within this Union according to their respective numbers. Census (through terminals) shall be conducted within two years after the first meeting of the Congress and within subsequent term of ten years, in such manner as they shall by Law direct.

When vacancies happen in the Representation from any State, the Executive Authority thereof shall issue Writs of Election to fill such vacancies.

The House of Representatives shall choose their Speaker (rotating presidency according to states alphabetical order) and other Officers (15, one by State) ; and shall have the sole power of Impeachment before the Senate.

Section 3.
The Senate of the United States of West Africa shall be composed of two Senators from each State, chosen by the Legislature thereof for six years and each Senator will have one vote. Immediately after they shall be assembled in consequence of the first Election, they shall be divided as equally as may be into three classes. The seats of the Senators of the first class shall be vacated at the expiration of the second year, of the second class at the expiration of the fourth year, so that one third may be chosen every second year ; and if vacancies happen by resignation or otherwise, during the recess of the the legislature of any State, the Executive thereof may make temporary appointments until the next meeting of the legislature which shall then fill such vacancies.

No person shall be a Senator who shall not have attained the age of thirty years, and been nine years a citizen of the United States of West Africa, and who shall not, when elected, be an inhabitant of that State for which he shall be chosen.

The Vice President of the United State of West Africa shall be President of the Senate, but shall have no vote, unless they be equally divided.

The Senate shall choose their other officers, and also a President pro tempore, in the absence of the Vice President of the United States of West Africa, or when he shall exercise the Office of President of the United States of West Africa.

The Senate will have the sole power to try all Impeachment. When sitting for that purpose, they shall be on oath or affirmation. When the President of the United States of West Africa is tried, the Chief Justice shall preside. And No person shall be convicted without the concurrence of two thirds of the members present.

Judgment in cases of Impeachment shall not extend further than to removal from office, and disqualification to hold and enjoy any office of honor, trust or profit under the United States of West Africa; but the party convicted shall nevertheless be liable and subject indictment trial, judgment and punishment according to Law.

Section 4.
The times, places and manner of holding Elections for senators and representatives, shall be prescribed in each State by the Legislature thereof, but the Congress may at any time by Law, make or alter such regulations, except as to the place of choosing Senators.

The Congress shall assemble at least once in every year, on the first monday in December, unless they shall by Law appoint a different day.

Section 5.
Each House shall be the judge of the Elections, Returns and Qualifications of its own members, and a majority of each shall constitute the Quorum to do business, but a smaller number may adjourn from day to day and may be authorized to compel the attendance of absent members, in such manners and under such penalties as each House may provide.

Each House may determine the rules of its proceedings, punish its members for disorderly behavior, and with the concurrence of two-thirds, expel a member.

Each House shall keep a Journal of its proceedings, and from time to time publish the same, excepting such parts as may in their judgment require secrecy, and the yeas and nays of the members of either House on any question shall, at the desire of one fifth of those present, be entered on the Journal.

Neither House, during the Session of Congress, shall, without the consent of the other, adjourn for more than three days, not to any other place than that in which the two Houses shall be sitting.

Section 6.
The Senators and Representatives shall receive a compensation for their services, to be ascertained by Law and paid out of the Treasury of the United States of West Africa.

They shall in all cases, except treason, felony and breach of the Peace, be privileged from arrest during their attendance at the Session of their respective Houses, and in going to and returning from the same; and for any speech or debate in either House, they shall not be questioned in any other place.

No Senator or Representative shall, during the time for which he was elected, be appointed to any civil office under the authority of the United States of West Africa which shall have been created, or the emoluments whereof shall have been increased during such time, and no person holding any office under the United States of West Africa, shall be a member of either House during his continuance in office.

Section 7.
All bills for raising revenue shall originate in the House of Representatives; but the Senate may propose or concur with amendments as on other Bills.

Every Bill which shall have passed the House of Representatives and the Senate, shall, before it become a Law, be presented to the President of the United States of West Africa; if he approves he shall sign it, but if not he shall return it with his objections to that House in which it shall have originated, who shall enter the objections at large on their Journal, and proceed to reconsider it. If after such reconsideration, two thirds of that House shall agree to pass the Bill, it shall be sent, together with the objections, to the other House, by which it shall likewise be reconsidered, and if approved by two thirds of that House, it shall become a Law. But in all such cases the votes of both Houses shall be determined by Yeas and Nays, and the names of the persons voting for and against the Bill shall be entered on the Journal of each House respectively. If any Bill shall not been returned by the President within ten days (Sundays excepted) after it shall have been presented to him, the same shall be a Law, in like manner as if he had signed it, unless the Congress by their adjournment prevent its return, in which case it shall not be a Law.

Every order, resolution, or vote to which the concurrence of the Senate and House of Representatives may be necessary (except on a question of Adjournment) shall be presented to the President of the United States of West Africa, and before the same shall take effect, the Senate and House of Representatives, according to the rules and limitations prescribed in the case of a Bill.

Section 8.

The Congress shall have power :
To lay and collect taxes, duties, Imposts and Exercises,
To pay the debts and provide for the common defence and General Welfare of the United States of West Africa but all duties, imposts and exercises shall be uniform throughout the United States of West Africa;
Borrow money on the credit of the United States of West Africa ;
Regulate commerce with Foreign Nations, and among the several states;
To establish an uniform rule of naturalization and uniform Laws on the subject of bankruptcies throughout The United States of West Africa;
To coin money, regulate the value thereof, and of foreign coin, and fix the standard of weights and measures;
To provide for the punishment of counterfeiting the securities and current coin of the United States of West Africa ;
To establish Post Offices and Post Roads;
To promote the progress of Science and useful Arts, by securing for limited times to authors and inventors the exclusive right to their respective writings and discoveries;
To constitute Tribunals inferior to the Supreme Court;

To define and punish Piracies and Felonies committed on the high Seas, and Offenses against the Law of Nations;

To negotiate as much as possible in order to avoid war,

To grant letters of marque and reprisal, and make rules concerning captures on land and water;

To raise and support armies, but no appropriation of money to that use shall be for a longer term than two years;

To create and maintain a Navy, that can be used for any purpose, including environmental problems;

To make rules for the government and regulation of the land and naval forces ;

To provide for calling forth the Militia to execute the laws of the Union, suppress insurrections and repel invasions;

To organize a one year (twelve months) military reserve-style model in which civic service would provide young people who have attained the legal age of 18, all activities including army, health, education, agriculture, public interest cleaning);

To provide for organizing, arming and disciplining the Militia, and for governing such part of them as may be employed the Service of the United States of West Africa, reserving to the States respectively, the appointment of the officers, and the authority of training the Militia according to the discipline prescribed by Congress ;

To exercise exclusive legislation in all cases whatsoever, over such district (not exceeding ten miles square) as may by cession of particular States, and the acceptance of Congress, become the seat of the government of the United states of West Afria, and to exercise like authority over places purchased by the consent of the legislature of the state in which the same shall be, for the erection of forts, magazines, arsenals, dockyards and other needful buildings;

And to make all laws which shall be necessary and proper for carrying into execution the foregoing powers, and all other powers vested by the Constitution in the Government of the United States of West Africa, or in any department or Officer thereof.

Section 9.
The migration or importation of such persons as any of the states now existing shall think proper to admit, shall not be prohibited by the Congress, but a tax or duty may be imposed on such importation not exceeding ten Dollars for each person. The privilege of the Writs of Habeas Corpus shall not be suspended, unless when in cases of rebellion or invasion the public safety may require it.

No Bill of Attainder or ex post facto law shall be passed.

No capitation, or other direct tax shall be laid, unless in proportion to the census herein before directed to be taken.

No tax or duty shall be laid on articles exported from any state.

No preferences shall be given by any regulation of commerce or revenue to the ports of one state over those of another nor shall vessels bound to, or fro, one state be obliged to enter, clear, or pay duties in another.

No money shall be drawn from the Treasury, but in consequence of appropriations made by law; and a regular statement and account of the receipts and expenditures of all public money shall be published from time to time.

No title of nobility shall be granted by the United States of West Africa ; and no person holding any office of profit or trust under them, shall, without the consent of the Congress, accept of any present, emolument, office, or title, of any kind whatever, from any king, prince or foreign state.

Section 10.
No state shall enter into any Treaty, Alliance, or Confederation, grant letters of Marque and Reprisal; coin money, emit bills of credit, make anything but gold and silver coin a tender in payment of debts; pass any bill of Attainder, ex post facto law, or law impairing the obligation of contracts, or grant any title of nobility.

No state shall, without the consent of the Congress, lay any taxes or duties on imports or exports, except what may be absolutely necessary for executing its inspection laws; and the net produce of all duties and imposts, laid by any state on imports or exports, shall be for the use of the Treasury, of the United States of West Africa, and all such laws shall be subject to the revision and control of the Congress.

No state shall, without the consent of Congress, lay any duty of Tonnage, keep troops, or ships of war in time of peace, enter into any agreement of compact with another state, or with a foreign power, or engage war, unless actually invaded, or in such imminent danger as will not admit of delay.

ARTICLE II

Section 1.

The executive Power shall be vested in the President of The United States of West Africa. He shall hold his office during the term of four years, and together with the Vice President chosen for the same term, be elected as follows :

Presidency shall alternate by state on the basis of alphabetical order state list. Vice-Presidency shall also alternate on the other way round.

The thirteen other positions according to their Importance in the protocol order, will be submitted to this rotation, so that each state will be represented at the head of federal organization.

The fifteen top executives shall be elected by direct universal suffrage, through terminals. Votes shall take place during 48 hours NON-STOP, immediately counted and automatically compiled to the organ in charge of publishing results.

Each state may organize primary elections under the same principle of alternate rotation, in order to choose their own candidates whose number shall not exceed three, the candidates shall be elected by universal suffrage for the sought position.

Each executive, in charge of one the highest federal position,

(President, Vice President, Speaker at the Congress,…), that is a candidate to his own position or to Another position, shall resign prior to the beginning of the following campaign.
To this end he shall be replaced by the deputy under Protocol order. No person is allowed to campaign while being in office, nor use in any way the state means for his own or personal interest. All candidates are equal in rights and citizenship.

Section 2.
The president shall be commander in chief of the Army and the Navy of the United States of West Africa, of the militia of the several states, when called into the actual service of federal states; he may require the opinion in writing, of the principal Officer in each of the executive departments, upon any subject related to the duties of their respective offices and he shall have power to grant reprieves and pardon for offenses against the United States, except in cases of « Impeachment ».

He shall have power, by and with the advice and consent of the Senate, to make treaties, provide two thirds of the Senators present concur; and he shall nominate, and by and with the advice and consent of the Senate, shall Appoint ambassadors, other public ministers and consuls, Judges of the Supreme Court, and all other officers of the United States of West Africa, whose appointments are not herein otherwise provided for, and which shall be Established by law.

But the Congress may by law vest the appointment of such inferior officers, as they think proper, in the President alone, in the courts of law, or in the Heads of departments.

The president shall have power to fill up all vacancies that May happen during the recess of the Senate by granting Commissions which shall expire at the end of their session.

Section 3.
The President shall from time to time give the Congress information of the state of the Union and recommend their consideration such measures as he shall judge necessary and expedient; he may, on extraordinary occasions, convene both Houses, or either of them, and in case of disagreement between them, with respect to the time of adjournment, he may adjourn them to such time as he shall think proper; he shall receive Ambassadors and other public ministers. He shall take care that the laws be faithfully executed and shall Commission all athe officers of the United States Of West Africa.

Section 4.
The President, Vice President and all civil officers of the United States of West Africa shall be removed from office on Impeachment for, and conviction of, treason, bribery or other high crimes and misdemeanors.

ARTICLE III

Section 1.
The Judicial power of the United States of West Africa shall be vested in one Supreme Court, and in such inferior Courts as the Congress may from time to time ordain and establish. The Judges, both of the Supreme and inferior Courts, shall

hold their offices during good behavior, and shall, at stated times receive for their services a compensation which shall not be diminished during their continuance in office.

Section 2.
The judicial power shall extend to all cases, in law and equity, arising under this Constitution, the laws of the United States of West Africa and treaties made, or which shall be made under their authority, to all cases affecting Ambassadors, other public Ministers and Consuls; to all cases of admiralty and maritime jurisdiction; to controversies to which the United States of West Africa shall be a party; to controversies between two or more States; between a State and citizens of another state; between citizens of different states, between citizens of the same state claiming lands under grants of different states, and between states, or the citizen thereof, and foreign states, citizens or subjects.

In all cases affecting ambassadors, other public Ministers and Consuls, and those in which a State shall be party, the Supreme Court shall have original jurisdiction.
In all other cases before mentioned, the Supreme Court shall have the Appellate Jurisdiction, both as to law and fact, with such exceptions, and un der regulations as the Congress shall make.

The trial of all crimes, except in cases of impeachment, shall be by Jury; and such trial shall be held in the state where the said crimes shall have been committed; but when not committed within any state, the trial shall be at such place or places as the Congress may by law have directed.

Section 3.
Treason against the United States of West Africa, shall consist only in levying war against them, or in adhering to their enemies, giving them aid and comfort.

No person shall be convicted of treason unless on the testimony of two witnesses to the same overt act, or on confession in open court.

The Congress shall have power to declare punishment of treason, but no attainder of treason shall work corruption of blood, or forfeiture except during the Life of the person attainted.

ARTICLE IV

Section 1.
Full faith and Credit shall be given in each state to the public acts, records, and judicial proceedings of every other state. And the Congress may by general laws prescribe the manner in with such acts, records and proceedings shall be proved, and the effect thereof.

Section 2.
The citizens of each state shall be entitled to all privileges and immunities of citizens in the several states.A person charged in any State with treason, felony, or other crimes, who shall flee from justice, and be found in another state, shall on demand of the Executive Authority of the state from

which he fled, be delivered up, to be removed to the state having jurisdiction of the crime.

No person held to Service or Labour in one State, under the laws thereof, escaping into another, shall, in consequences of any law or regulation therein, be discharged from such service or labour, but shall be delivered up on claim of the Party to whom such Service or Labour may be due.

Section 3.

New states may be admitted by the Congress into this Union; but no new state shall be formed or erected within the jurisdiction of any other state, nor any state formed by the junction of two or more states, without the consent of the legislature of the states concerned as well as of the Congress.

The Congress shall have power to dispose of and make all needful rules and regulations respecting the territory or other property belonging to the United States of West Africa, and nothing in this Constitution shall be so construed as to prejudice any claims of the United States of West Africa, or of any particular state.

Section 4.

The United States of West Africa shall guarantee to every state in this Union a republican form of government, and shall protect each of them against invasion; and on application of the legislature, or of the Executive (when the legislature cannot be convened) against domestic violence.

ARTICLE V

The Congress, whenever two thirds of both Houses shall deem it necessary, shall propose amendments to this Constitution, or, on the application of the Legislatures of two thirds of the several states, shall call a convention for proposing amendments, which in either case, shall be valid to all intents and purposes, as part of this Constitution, when ratified by the legislatures of three fourths of the several states, or by conventions, in three fourths thereof, as the one or the other mode of ratification may be proposed by the Congress, provided that no amendments shall in any manner affect the first and fourth clauses in the ninth section of the first article; and that no state, without its consent, shall be deprived of its equal suffrage in the Senate.

ARTICLE VI

All debts contracted and engagements entered into, before the adoption of this Constitution, shall be as valid against the United States of West Africa under this Constitution as under the Confederation.

This Constitution, and the laws of the United States of West Africa which shall be made in pursuance thereof; and all treaties made, or which shall be made, under the Authority of the United States of West Africa, shall be the supreme Law of the Lan; and the judges in every State shall be bound thereby, anything in the Constitution or Laws of any State to the contrary notwithstanding.

The Senators and Representatives before mentioned, and the members of the several states legislatures, and all executive and judicial officers, both of the United States of West Africa and of the several states, shall be bound by Oath or Affirmation, to support this Constitution; but no religious Test shall ever be required as a qualification to any office or public trust under the United States of West Africa.

ARTICLE VII

The Ratification of the Convention of nine States out of fifteen, shall be sufficient for the establishment of this constitution between the States so ratifying the same.

Done in Convention by the Unanimous Consent of the Congress

In Witness whereof
We have hereunto subscribed our Names

SUGGESTED AMENDMENTS

ARTICLE I

Congress shall make no law respecting an establishment of religion, or prohibiting the free exercise thereof; or abridging the freedom of speech, or of the press, or the right of the people peaceably to assemble, and to petition the Government for a redress of grievances.

ARTICLE II

A well regulated Militia, being necessary to the security of a free state, the right of the people to keep and bear arms, for their own defence shall be determined by the Public force under the terms of the rule of law.

ARTICLE III

No soldier shall, in time of peace, be quartered in any House, without the consent of the owner, nor in time of war, but in a manner to be prescribed by law.

ARTICLE IV

The right of the people to be secure in their persons, houses, papers, and effects, against unreasonable searches and seizures, shall both be violated, and no warrants shall be issued but upon probable cause, supported by Oath or affirmation, and particularly describing the place to be searched, and the persons or things to be seized.

ARTICLE V

No person shall be held to answer for a capital, or otherwise infamous crime, unless on a presentment or indictment of a Grand Jury, except in cases arising in the land or naval forces, or in the Militia, when in actual service in time of war or public danger; nor shall any person be subject for the same offence to be twice put in jeopardy of life or limb; nor shall be compelled in any criminal case to be a witness against himself, nor be deprived of life, liberty, or property, without due process of law; nor shall private property be taken for public use, without just compensation.

ARTICLE VI

In all prosecutions, the accused will enjoy the right to a speedy and public trial, by an impartial jury of the state and district wherein the crime shall have been committed, which district shall have been previously ascertained by law, and to be informed of the nature and cause of the accusation; to be confronted with the witnesses against him; to have compulsory process for obtaining witnesses in his favor, and to have the assistance of Counsel for his defense.

ARTICLE VII

In suits at common law, where the value in controversy shall exceed twenty dollars, the right of trial shall be preserved, and no fact tried by a jury, shall be otherwise re-examined in any court of the United States of West Africa, than according to the rules of the common law.

ARTICLE VIII

Excessive bail shall not be required, nor excessive fines imposed, nor cruel and unusual punishments inflicted.

ARTICLE IX

The enumeration in the Constitution, of certain rights, shall not be construed to den or disparage others retained by the people.

ARTICLE X

The powers not delegated to the United States of West Africa by the constitution, nor prohibited by it to the states, are reserved to the States respectively, or to the people.

ARTICLE XI

The judicial power of the United States shall not be construed to extend to any suit in law or equity, commenced or prosecuted against one of the United States of West Africa by citizens of another state, or by citizens of subjects of any foreign state.

ARTICLE XII

The electors shall meet in their respective states, and vote by ballot for President and Vice President, one of whom, at least, shall not be an inhabitant of the same state with themselves; they shall name in their ballots the person voted for as President, and in distinct ballots the person voted for as Vice President and of the number of votes for each, which lists they shall sign and certify, and transmit sealed to the seat of the government of the United States of West Africa, directed to the President of the Senate.The President of the

Senate shall, in the presence of the Senate and the House of Representatives, open all the certificates and the votes shall be counted. The person having the greatest number of votes for President, shall be the President, if such number be a majority, then from the persons having the highest numbers not exceeding three on the list of those voted for as President, the House of Representatives shall choose immediately, by ballot, the President but in choosing the President, the votes shall be taken by states, the representation from each state having one vote; a quorum for this purpose shall consist of a member or members from two-thirds of the states, and a majority of all the states shall be necessary to a choice. And if the House of Representatives shall not choose a President whenever the right of choice shall devolve upon them, before the fourth day of March next following, then the Vice President shall act as President, as in the case of the death or other constitutional disability of the President.

The person having the greatest number of votes as Vice President, shall be the Vice President, if such number be a majority of whole number of electors appointed, and if no person have a majority, then from the two highest numbers on the list, the Senate shall choose the Vice President; a quorum for the purpose shall consist of 24, which shall represent two-thirds of the whole number of senators, and a majority of the whole number shall be necessary to a choice.

But no person constitutionally inelegible to the office of President shall be eligible to that of Vice President of the United States of West Africa.

ARTICLE XIII

Section 1.

Neither slavery nor involuntary servitude, except as a punishment for crime whereof the party shall have been duly convicted, shall exist within the United States of West Africa, or any place subject to their jurisdiction. The federal state shall investigate on every suspicious case of servitude especially of youngsters under the age of majority, that may have been sold as payment for incurred family debts.

ARTICLE XIV

Section 1.

All persons born or naturalized in the United States of West Africa, and subject to the jurisdiction thereof, are citizens of the United States of West Africa and of the
State wherein they reside. No state shall make or enforce any law which abridge the privileges or immunities of citizens of the United States of West Africa; nor shall
any state deprive any person of life, liberty, or property, without due process of law; nor deny to any person within its jurisdiction the equal protection of the laws.

Section 2.

No person shall be a Senator or Representative in Congress, or elector of President and Vice President, or hold any office, civil or military, under the United States of West Africa, or under any state, who, having previously taken an

oath, as a member of Congress, or as an officer of the United States of West Africa, or as a member of any state legislature, or as an executive or judicial officer of any state, to support the
constitution of the United States of West Africa, shall have engaged in insurrection or rebellion against the same, or given aid or comfort to the enemies thereof. But Congress may vote of two thirds of each House, remove such disability.

Section 3.
The validity of the public debt of the United States of West Africa, authorized by law, including debts incurred for payments of pensions and bounties for services in suppressing.

But neither the United States of West Africa nor any state shall assume or pay any debt or obligation incurred in aid of insurrection or rebellion against the United States of West Africa, or any claim for the loss or emancipation of any slave; but all such debts, obligations and claims shall be held illegal and void.

ARTICLE XV

Section 1.
The right of citizens of the United States of West Africa to vote shall not be denied or abridged by the United States or by any state on account of race, color, or previous condition of servitude.

ARTICLE XVI

The Congress shall have power to lay and collect taxes on incomes, from whatever source derived, without apportionment among the several states, and without regard to any census or enumeration.

ARTICLE XVII

Section 1.
The Senate of the United States of West Africa shall be composed of two Senators from each state, elected by the people thereof, for six years through terminal and confirmed by ballot.

Section 2.
When vacancies happen in the representation of any state in the Senate, the executive authority of such state shall issue writs of election to fill such vacancies provided that the legislature of any state may empower the executive thereof to make temporary appointments until the people fill the vacancies by election as the legislature may direct.

Section 3.
This amendment shall not be so construed as to affect the election or term of any senator chosen before it becomes valid as part of the Constitution.

ARTICLE XVIII

The right of citizens of the United States of West Africa to vote shall not be denied or abridged by the United States of West Africa or by any state on account of gender.
Congress shall have power to enforce this article by appropriate legislation.

ARTICLE XIX

Section 1.
The terms of the President and Vice President shall end at noon on the 20th day of May, and the terms of Senators and Representatives at noon on the third day of May, of the years in which such terms would have ended if this article had not been ratified; and the terms of their successors shall then begin.

Section 2.
The Congress shall assemble at least once in every year, and such meeting shall begin at noon on the third day of May, unless they shall by law appoint a different day.

Section 3.
If, at the time fixed for the beginning of the term of the President, the President elect shall have died, the Vice President elect shall become President.

If a President shall not have been chosen before the time fixed for the beginning of this term, or if the President elect shall have failed to qualify, then the Vice President elect shall act as President until a President shall have qualified, declaring who shall then act as President, or in the manner in which one who is to act shall be selected, and such person shall act accordingly until a President or Vice President shall have qualified.

Section 4.

The Congress may by law provide for the case of the death of any of the persons from whom the House of Representatives may choose a President whenever the right of choice shall have devolved upon them.

ARTICLE XX

Section 1.

No person shall be elected to the office of the President more than twice, and no person who has held the office of President, or acted as President, for more than two years of a term to which some other person was elected President shall be elected to the office of the President more than once. But this article shall not apply to any person holding the office of President, when this article was proposed by the Congress, and shall not prevent any person who may be holding the office of President, or acting as President during the term within which this article becomes operative from holding the office of President or acting as President during the remainder of such term.

Section 2.

This article shall be inoperative unless it shall have beenratified as an amendment to the Constitution by the Legislatures of three fourths of the several states within seven years from the date of its submission to the states by the Congress.

ARTICLE XXI

Section 1.

The right of citizens of the United States of West Africa to vote in any primary or other election for President or Vice President, for electors for President or Vice President, or for Senator or Representative in Congress, shall not be denied or abridged by the United States of West Africa or any state by reason of failure to pay any poll tax or other tax.

Section 2.

The Congress shall have power to enforce this article by appropriate legislation.

ARTICLE XXII

Section 1.

In case of the removal of the President from office or of his death or resignation, the Vice President shall become President.

Section 2.

Whenever there is a vacancy in the office of Vice President, the President shall nominate a Vice President who shall take office upon confirmation by a majority vote of both Houses of Congress.

Section 3.

Whenever the President transmits to the President pro tempore of the Senate and the Speaker of the House of Representatives his written declaration that he is unable to discharge the powers and duties of his office, and until he transmits to them a written
declaration to the contrary, such powers and duties shall be discharged by the Vice President as acting President.

Section 4.

Whenever the Vice President, and a majority of either the principal officers of the executive departments or of such other body as Congress may by law provide, transmit to the President pro tempore of the Senate and the speaker of the House of Representatives their written declaration that the President is unable to discharge the powers and duties of the office as Acting President.

Thereafter, when the President transmits to the President **pro tempore** of the Senate and the speaker of the House of Representatives his written declaration that no inability exists, he shall resume the powers and duties of his office unless the Vice President and a majority of either the principal officers of the executive department or of such other body as Congress may by law provide, transmit within four days to the President pro tempore of the Senate and the speaker of the House of Representatives their written declaration that the President is unable to discharge the powers and duties of his office. Thereupon Congress shall decide the issue, assembling within forty eight hours for that purpose if not in session. If the Congress, within twenty one day after receipt of the latter written declaration, or if Congress is not in session, within twenty one days after Congress is required to assemble, determined by two third vote of both Houses that the President is unable to discharge the powers and duties of this office, the Vice President shall resume the powers and duties of his office.

ARTICLE XXIII

Section 1.
The right of citizens of the United States of West Africa, who are eighteen years of age or older, to vote shall not be denied or abridged by the United States or by any state on account of their age.

ARTICLE XXIV

No law, varying the compensation for the services of the Senators and Representatives, shall take effect, until an election of Representatives shall have interv.

3. The starry golden spiral, the flag, and its meaning.

Performing a simulation of the United States of West Africa flag (the starry golden spiral) with its rainbow colors (USOWA)

The USOWA flag is a flag in 10/19 proportion often called "Stars on Gold Spiral" or "starry golden with rainbow colors".

It is represented with 16 zones of rainbow colors, going from the centre to the spiral edges, framed with three lines (red, yellow and blue).
Right in the middle of each zone and even within the golden spiral line, one can find 15 five edged stars, in golden progression. The 15 starred zones stand for the 15 founding member states united to create the United States of West Africa. The 16th zone represents an open way towards the rest of Africa in view of implementing the African federal state.

Each zone is meant to be sewn one to another (and not Imprinted) so that to symbolize the sealing of the Union existing between each founding member state.

The golden spiral has a partial "eadem mutata resurgo" characteristic, which means that is O center remains the same from π et d'angle $\pi/2$; it is thus nearly a logarithmic spiral with m defined by $e_{m\pi/2} = $ phi,

a polar equation $\rho = a\,\varphi^{\frac{\theta}{\pi/2}}$ going through points A, A', A"
etc...

Every time it goes round the golden spiral radius is multiplied
by $\varphi^4 \simeq 6,9$; the tangential polar angle constant value is

$$\psi = \operatorname{arc\,cot}\left(\frac{2}{\pi}\ln\varphi\right) \simeq 73°$$

The USOWA flag shows the divine proportion which result
will be in proportion with the law of the universe.

4. This partially united Africa motto

In God we stay !

Such is the motto of the United States of West Africa –
USOWA-, and the whole of Africa.

Whether one believes or not in God is not the point for dark
pigmented people, because they are <u>light carriers</u> when it
comes to their wide capability in storing and synthesizing
daylight.

They are digging in order to find ways to express body (its
mortal condition), and this is soundly praised through the
Cosmic harmony. We stay in and with him. Just a sparkle of
the divine conscience comes to admire the work, the garden
of splendors, the expressed universe we are able to see when
we look at the sun.

That is the way God made everything, in divine proportion
(gold number), with a quality in vibration corresponding in
numbers to the Hierarchy of beings and things, according
 to the Work plan.

This has already been integrated in his residual memory so
that he sees to it that :

- they will not stoop to the level of beast (cruelty), though he
usually react the same way animals' body do.

- mating with animals is a totally forbidden transgression. There can be no archetypal hybridization thanks to natural selection.

- they will not destroy their habitation (the earth) due to an insatiable hunger for earthy goods.

- they will not put an end to the species diversity.

- they will not forget that men are sun worshippers, the very source of life.

5. The anthem of the Light carriers

Aton Anthem, psalm, this anthem is said to have been written by Amenhotep IV / Akhenaton.

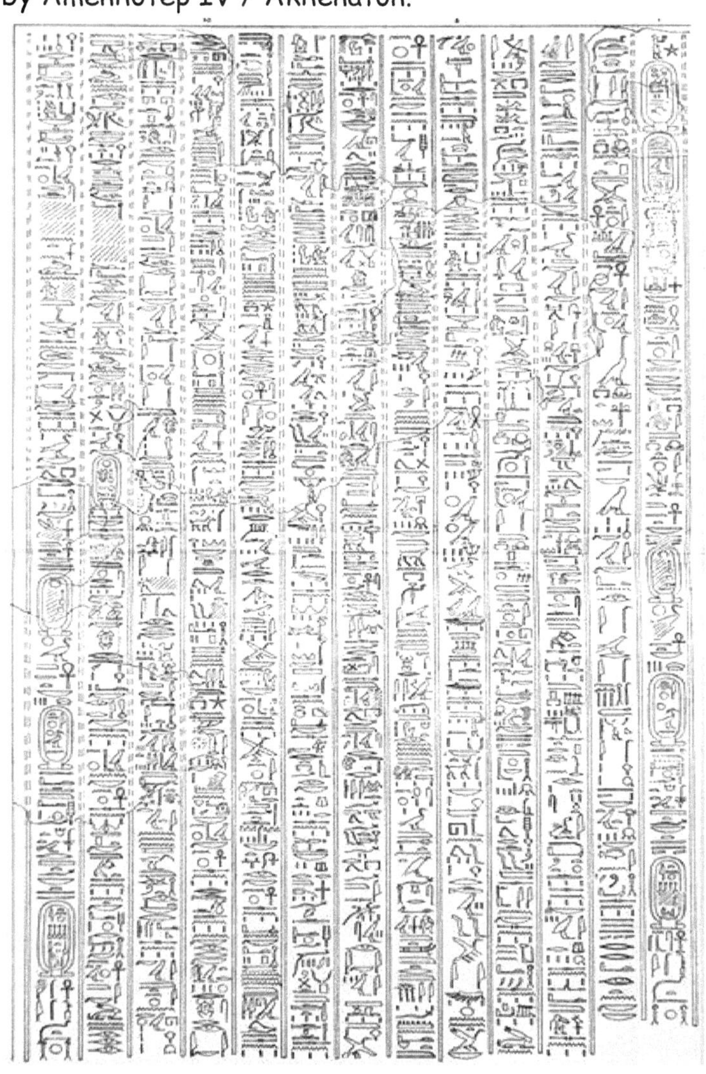

- Line 1 :

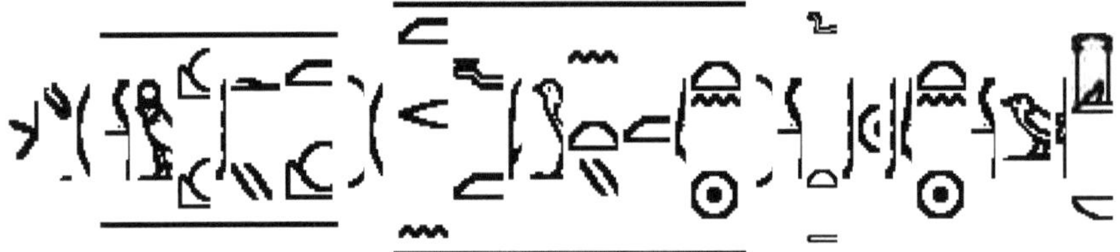

- Line 2 :

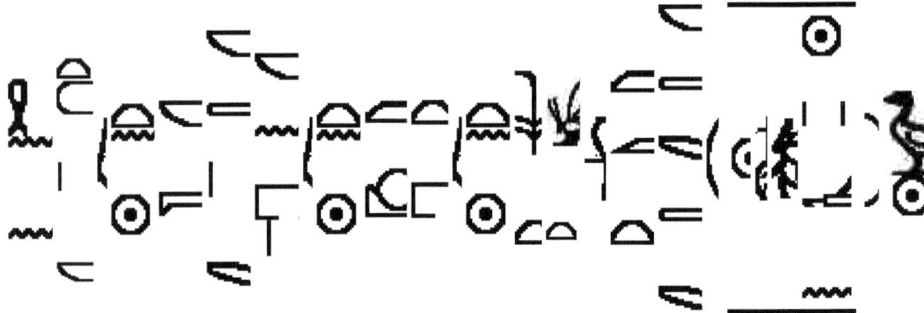

- Line 3 :

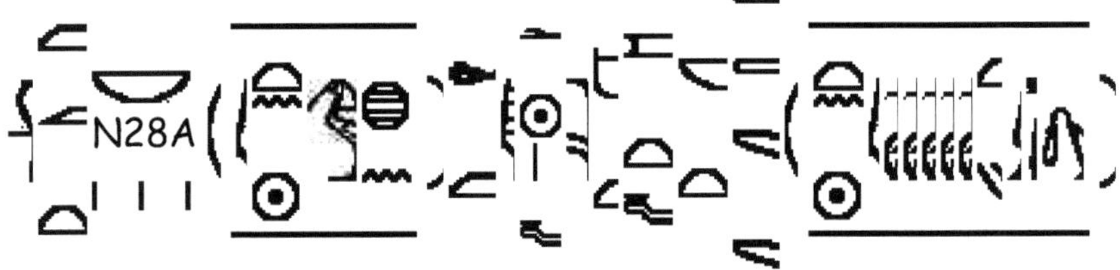

Line 4 :

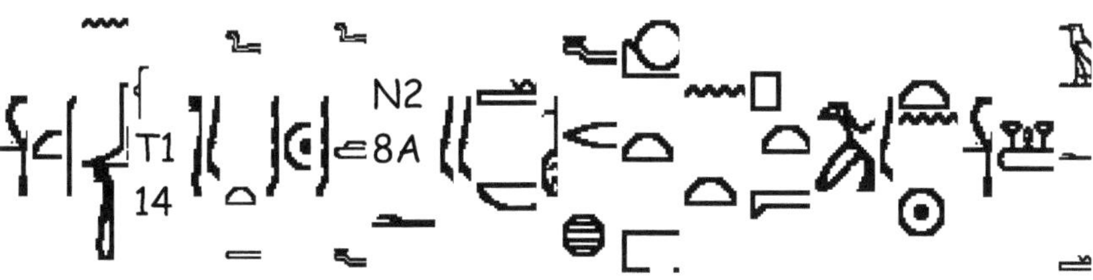

Line 5 :

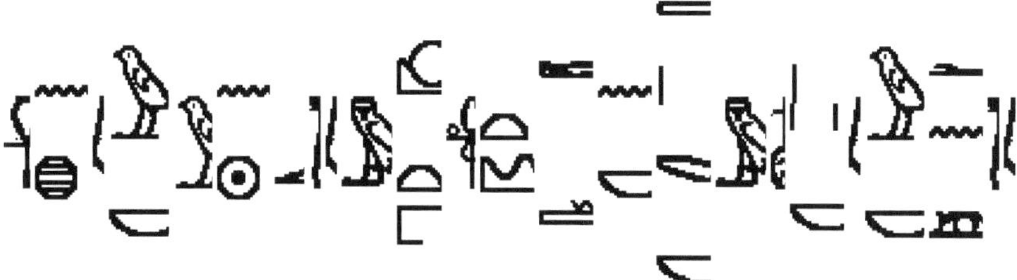

Line 6 :

Line 7 :

- Line 8 :

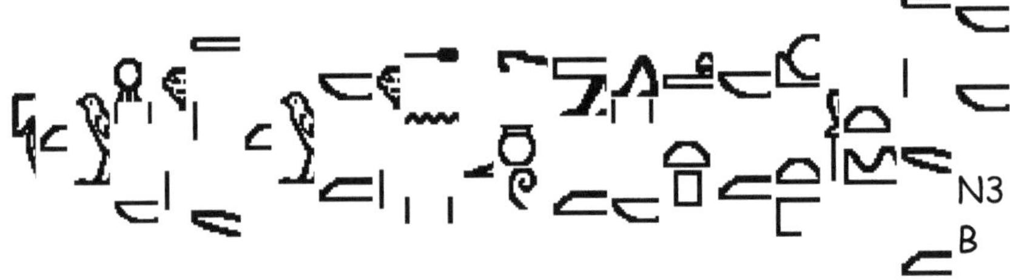

- Line 9 :

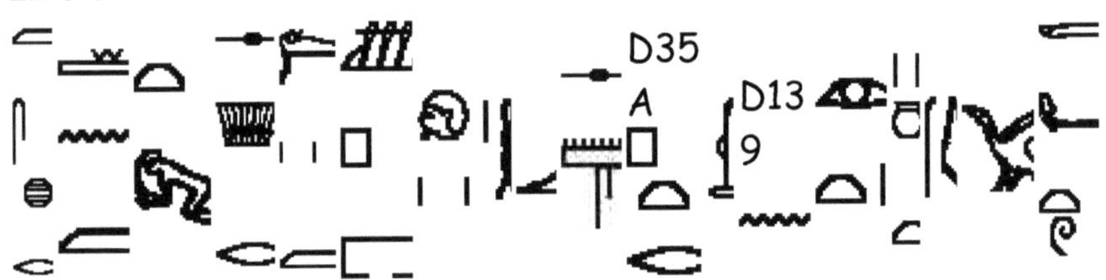

- Line 10 :

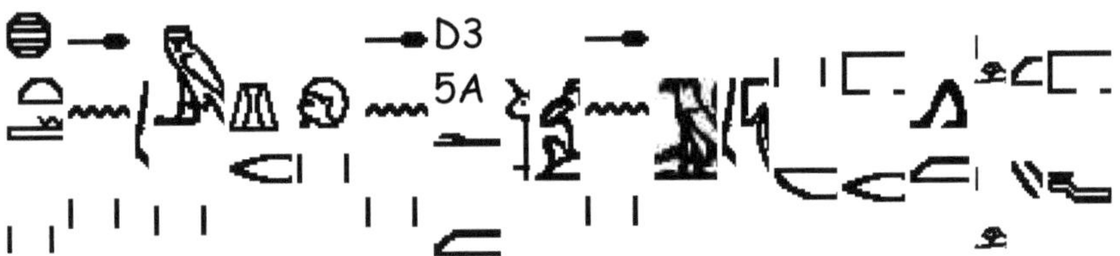

- Line 11 :

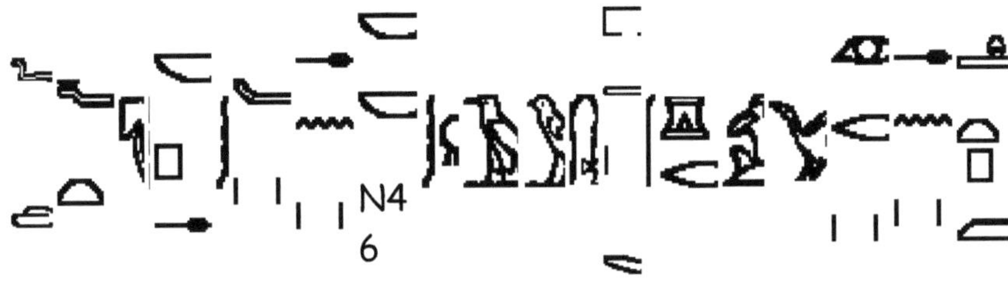

- Line 12 :

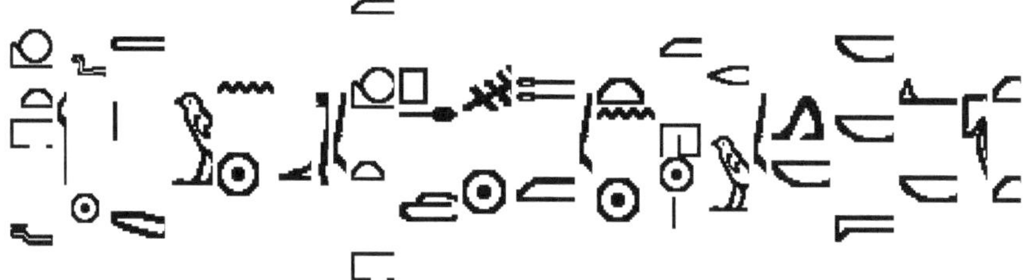

- Line 13 :

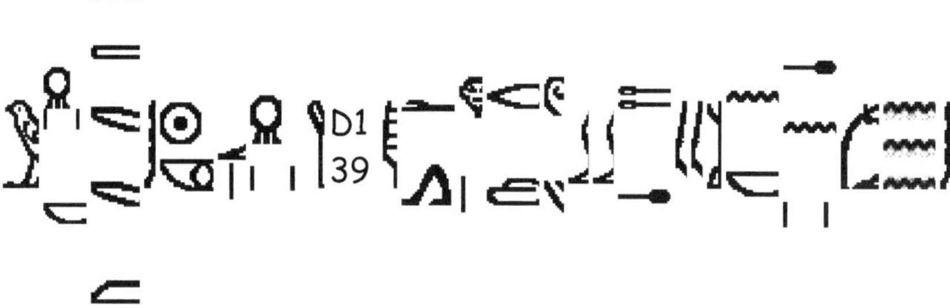

- Line 14 :

USOWA Anthem (from Aton Akhenaton)
Hymne des USOWA (from the hymn to Aton of Akhenaton)

You rise beautifully in the skyline,
Living Sun, who has been there since the beginning
You shine in the Eastern skyline
Every country is filled with your beauty
You are beautiful, great, bright, you Rise above every country,
All of them being embraced to the outer confines of your universe.

(The audience chants the refrain)

Mmm Mmm Mmm   Mmm Mmm Mmm   Mmm Mmm Mmm   Mmm

Eééh éééh éééh   éééh éééh éééh   éééh éééh éééh   éééh

Oôô oôôo ôôô   ôôô ôôô ôôô   ôôô ôôô ôôô   ôôô

They have wholly surrendered to you Re,
 All of them linked one to another for the sake of your beloved Son.
Although you are far away, your rays get to the earth
You are the men's whole face, we know nothing of your venues.
When you lie in the West, under the skyline,
The earth lies shadowy, as if dead..
At dawn, you shine in the horizon, all enlightened by you, the sun ;

(The audience chants the refrain)

Mmm Mmm Mmm   Mmm Mmm Mmm   Mmm Mmm Mmm   Mmm

Eééh éééh éééh   éééh éééh éééh   éééh éééh éééh éééh

Oôô oôô ôôô   ôôô ôôô ôôô   ôôô ôôô ôôô   ôôô

At daytime, darkness is driven off by your rays.
The fifteen countries wake up lively, men get on their feet,
Thanks to you, they clean up their bodies, put their clothes
on;

Open their arms in adoration with your wakening,
The entire earth is at work.

(The audience chants the refrain)

Mmm Mmm Mmm   Mmm Mmm Mmm   Mmm Mmm Mmm   Mmm

Eééh éééh éééh   éééh éééh éééh   éééh éééh éééh éééh

Oôô oôô ôôô   ôôô ôôô ôôô   ôôô ôôô ôôô   ôôô

You give spirit to whatever created by you
So mysterious to our eyes are your creations !
Your heart created the earth, although you were all alone,
Putting each man where they belong
With their own different languages,
Special characteristics and skin colors ;
Wherever you can be far away or very near,

(The audience chants the refrain)

Mmm Mmm Mmm   Mmm Mmm Mmm   Mmm Mmm Mmm   Mmm

Eééh éééh éééh   éééh éééh éééh   éééh éééh éééh   éééh

Oôô oôôo ôôô   ôôô ôôô ôôô   ôôô ôôô ôôô   ôôô

Posture of the citizen during the anthem

While singing the hymn, the citizens of the United States of West Africa show their attachment to the ideals of their nation by holding their hands and arms open over their heads (as shown on the photo above), and chant during refrains.

Kemetic Sun Salutation is partially done (position 1 et position 11)
Hands are joined and put right before the face, then arms are lifted over the head, with open palms towards the sky, so that the whole body be ready to receive the sublime fragrance.

ENCHAÎNER LA SÉQUENCE

The 21th century shall be either spiritual or non existent (nuclear destruction). Every morning this chant may be recited prior to the 'Sun salutation' , with the left hand on the heart and the right hand index lifted right in the middle of the forehead.

I am grateful my Lord for the return of my own consciousness.
I am grateful my Lord that you gave me the privilege to participate, one more day to the fulfillment of your plans in order to pursue my own personal change at this stage of comprehension.

Keep me endlessly in touch with your own conscience and grant me the privilege to receive whatever necessary inspiration. Let that be! !

6. PanAfrican emergencies

September 14, 2019 challenge against the agreement of ECO currency to the euro, which result ipso facto to the extension of the CFA zone to the other African countries is absolutely legitimate, because the euro is a far too strong

Currency for the economy of African countries. The fake stability of fixed parity will only destroy their growth. Although having been set free the former slaves do not wish to leave the original comfort, of the farm, they will rather choose to be paid for their work. The slave owners are working on it.

The second emergency challenge is to say NO TO NUCLEAR plants in Africa. The energy potential (hydroelectricity, wind, sun, sea et gas) is so GIGANTIC, that Africa has
 no need whatsoever to import the nuclear danger at so high a cost. The ultimate goal of these nuclear plants that are proposed to some African countries is to have a place to store China and Russia nuclear wastes.

De-forestation and the selling of our lands are real emergency challenges that should mobilize our citizens to be organized wildly in Africa against that.

Anticipation

Black people remain way too emotional when it comes to implement this challenge.

They need to think "coldly" and anticipate in how to make a long term strategy real. African and Pan African people ambitions and ideals must be firmly defined. Kemi Seba can lead the way and be our powerful voice.

The echo of the clamoring ECO bell, in Africanists collective unconsciousness, is to put an end to existing micro-states and kinglets for good.

Anticipation 1 : Symbolic creation of : USOWA (USWA)

UNITED STATES OF WEST AFRICA

Produce a comprehensive report of the texts (constitution) and all symbols related to the federal state (flag, coat of arms, etc.) which will be symbolic declaration of the birth of USOWA and inauguration of the moral authority that shall represent the nation wherever needed.

USOWA is an embryonic stage leading to the birth of the United States of West Africa, which be following the effective implementation of a comprehensive free trade area within the continent (FTAC).

This USOWA safe box (USWA) shall be sent to every citizen/political party/association/government of West Africa. The content will be recorded and displayed on line www.yékola-Sobëgge-liguéy.org for free audio distribution. The coming generation needs to be mentally ready for a federal state USOWA-USWA.

Anticipation 2 : Creation of African gold reserves

No federal state can exist without its own currency (The European Union, the United States of America). It is imperative to convince the President of Ghana, Nana AKUFO to let private societies (Dansote, Avon,) bearing favorably recommended government permit, transmit the FSA(ECOWAS Financial Service Agency), wait to get the receipt of formal agreement for the creation of the African Gold Reserves and Deposit and Consignation Office.

This private business shall buy at a preferential rate (Pan African agreement for producer states) the gold produced in the whole African continent. The main ambition
Of this Office will be to progressively constitute gold reserves to ultimately get the same amount of gold that USA/FED in roughly 5 to 10 years.

<u>How?</u>
Kemi powerful voice will spread all over the continent to make every panafricanist contribute one dollar a day which make 360 dollars per inhabitant for a 500 million
People continent, all of them shareholders, and bearer of shares.

The public's subscriptions will be received through mobile money offices opened in every country not to mention the private wealthy people or middle class, or interested countries, or people in the whole wide world that are eager to invest funds.

The powerful voice of Kemi shall call all African gold producers to sell their gold tax-free to the Office at better price; a highly positive sovereignty exercise.

In the first place, deposits and consignation will constitute the main activity of the office until the proper amount of gold reserves is attained, prior to becoming the USOWA sole currency incubator and consequently the reference rate with the agreement of the secondary central banks.

Anticipation 3. Dissemination of Knowledge in African languages

VOCALIZING all the knowledge accumulated by humanity in order to make it available to every African in every spoken language throughout Africa, starting with wolof language.

With the new technologies and learning modes, the oral method which is widely spread and used in Africa will facilitate the acquisition of knowledge for the African people.

Facilitate the access of academic knowledge to the greater number of young people, through oral books, oral lessons in schools and universities throughout Senegal and ultimately West Africa.

Provide free access to talking books through the platform, by using a smartphone application and the internet. Widely spread the use of oral/spoken text books (lessons and exercises included), with programs implemented by the ministry of National Education for every country concerned, for primary, secondary and university level.

Provide every library of every school with paper books so that parents will not have to make anymore expense for academic books.

Prepare the education of an academic elite, a qualified workforce in order for them to be ready and available whenever companies need of them due to the induced economic upturn; in conformity with sustainable development goals.

Anticipation 4 and 5. Fresh water and arable Lands resources

Produce and carry fresh water throughout the continent towards dried lands, after desalination.

Why do we sell our arable lands to the Chinese or anyone else? Kemi Seba powerful voice is once again going to be raised and tell everything about these enormous deals taking place in each and every country.

Anticipation 6

Abundant production of electricity with locally refined minerals.
Locally refined minerals have two major benefits :
1. local extraction and transformation reduce environmental impact
2. better production costs

Anticipation 7

A desirable future for humanity added to a good strategy as regards this future.

When it comes to build up Africa, we African people (kamites) are talking about the desirable future of Humanity on the whole.

The good strategy is to associate our human brothers, the indo-europeans (white people actually) for three reasons ;
- there is only one human race ethnically divided in three
 main groups (black, white and yellow)
- facilitate the integration of white people in a black continent in order to teach them what universal brotherhood is about without their being obsessed by total domination
And work together for a better comprehension of the scales values for the protection of our commonly shared habitacle; the earth.
- No one is going to a B planet, after having destroyed our earth. The people who favour the rise of "aryans" are surely working for their own domination, but the natural selection rate taking place in the hybrids remains static (25 %).

- The great replacement has no chance to take place (Noah's arch for the preservation of all kind of species) all our energy must be focused on creating instead of contesting about easily solved problems. May God help to us to be not only outstanding warriors (enduring, persevering and resilient), but open to listen and understand things the right way in order to build new Humanity.

Yôga Yôga Yôga (listen, liste, listen)
Azambé, â Zambé, Azambé (God and his numerous manifestations)
Ngui lè mbé, (so I talked, so I said, say the 'akoua' from northern Congo B)

7. Backbone and foundations of the federal state

The pillars and foundations are :

They are the political and citizens who will create :

- The constitution, the flag and the motto of the federal state USOWA (USWA) by the civil society, shall symbolize the way to alleviate things.

Economic sovereignty

- The Golden Reserves Office of Deposits and Consignation
- Wari-Wara, the sole currency, with the guaranty of the Federal gold reserves.
Cultural independence(getting away from the chains of mental slavery)
- Matatu, the search engine, with African culture content
- building a replica of the Saqqara pyramid (same size than the ooriginal), in the moutains between Sequoue and Parakou ; a special place for a rise at spiritual and scientific level.
- building smaller replicas of Saqqara pyramid in each state member of the Union in order for them to become connecting places at spiritual and scientific level.

The vision
The building of the desirable future of humanity, Africa.

The building of this Africa will be real

- In bringing fresh water to arid lands inside the continent, following desalination, so as to quantify, what needed vegetables and fruit trees are to be planted in order to provide food security and support the citizens purchase power.

- Promoting ecology through recycling ; exhaustive waste recycling and enhancing metal recycling and re-using due to the coming rarefaction of metals, cleaning of oceans, rivers and cities.

- Maintaining group forests systems, through massive reforestation

Wood operation on reforested spaces;

- Being extremely wary before the nuclear danger despite the energy potential;

- Local transformation of minerals ; thus limiting the environmental impact and lower production costs of materials derived from minerals extracted on our continent;

- Make sure that our continent remains a melting-pot for all ethnical groups (black, white, yellow) as there is only one human race, despite the color differences due to melanin.

7.1. Detailed explanations about the Africa gold reserves

I. CREATION OF THE GOLD RESERVES OFFICE OF DEPOSITS AND CONSIGNATIONS (AGRODC)

A number of knowledgeable persons and informed businessmen are going to create the African Gold Reserves Office of Deposits and Consignations under the auspices of the President of Ghana, with headquarter based at Accra.

The project is written and introduced according to the rules and regulations in place, validated by the government
of Ghana, and shall be forwarded to the Community authorities like COSUMAF in view of getting the agreement of the providers of financial services.

II. OBJECTIVES

- the fundamental mission is to put together the more important gold reserves of the continent, by buying them all. This should take about 10 years to gather
10 000 tons of gold coming from Africa.

- one of the greatest measures to be undertaken concerning Public debt is to make a separation between the daily backlog service department to allocate amortization.

- it is a deposit and guarantee office which role is to guarantee the payment of pending obligations, contribute to debt amortization, and incidentally contribute to the implementation of the federal reserve (creation of the single African currency).

III. Panafrican federative cash operations

Despite being a private office, there still is a need to create a member states credit for African countries;
- the best way being to ensure a regular debt service
- a regular amortization exercise, by partly mitigating every year the public debt, offering a guarantee to creditors for the interests annual service and also the capital refund of their debts, provided that well-assured amortization services be placed at the top of the agenda of public charges.

The Public Redemption Fund is responsible for every operation concerning the amortization of public debt, as a guarantee fund, for the reimbursement of obligations undertaken par general receivers and that would have been repaid by them ; for the bonds general accounting, their refund according to the laws, and the distribution of allocated interests.

-As a deposit office, from the consignations department for the whole continent;
- as a deposit for the placement in accumulation of disused military effects
- placement in accumulation of deductions made on employees

salaries, consolidate to create pension funds, public administration, or their conversion at 5 %.
- placement of open source products, of communal assets deposits, of deposits of 10 %
of the communal assets income tax, allocated to religious matters, and personnel to create begging's places, deposits of products on grains.

Next Chronogramme
2020 : Private project for the constitution of gold reserves of Africa
2020 : Private project for the search engine with african content
2020 : Formal and symbolic creation, of the USOWA federal state Interim implementation of federal institutions

7.2 Just a word on the single currency of the federal state

Name of currency : Wari-Wara

Parity : floating, up to 1/3 of dollar

Guarantee : gold reserves and currencies constitution in equal or superior value and quantity to that of the United States of America Federal Bank.

7.3. The search engine with African content

PRIVATE PROJECT

Matatu

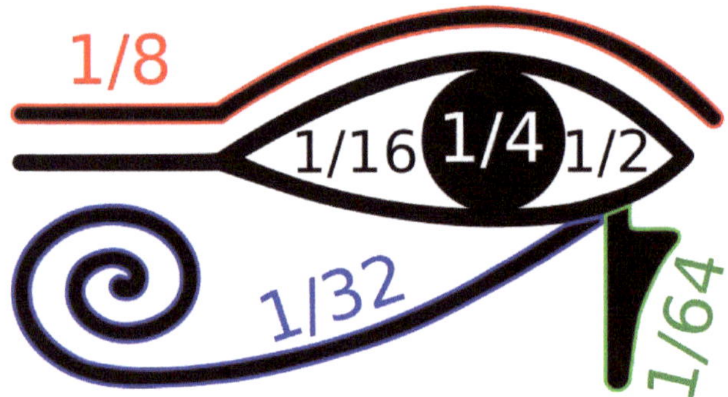

Mail address Maat-Matatu

Mmail ou Maatmail

8. Action taken to build the desirable future for Humanity

With all the mining resources, the amazing energetic potential and the strong young demography of the continent, are the African people able to build this desirable future for Humanity ? Once the federal state has financed the FRESH WATER Project « production and transportation of fresh water to the arid lands situated inside Africa, right after desalination of sea water», each citizen will be guaranteed at least the minimum of a purchase power.

Food security will not depend anymore on imports, nor emergency aid or whether hazards, because the presence of water in these arid lands will ensure an all year long agricultural production instead of 2 months a year.

The entire production of gold within the continent has to be bought in order to constitute the USOWA federal state gold reserve, the objective being to gather 10 thousand tons of gold.

The geographical distribution of the USOWA bodies and works headquarter.
- the gold reserves and the deposit and consignation Office at ACCRA ;
- The Senate at ABUJA
- The House of Representatives at Ouagadougou
- The federal capital city at Freetown (Sierra Leone)
- The pyramid of Saqqara's replica in Benin

Appendix

Press Release
Fresh water project (Senegal & Africa Digest excerpt)
Kaolack Liquefied gas terminal
University poles

Press Release

We are informing the public from ECOWAS area about

THE ORGANIZATION OF CIVIL SOCIETY AND CITIZEN DAYS
AT (ACCRA), (COTONOU) and (OUAGADOUGOU)
from February 12th to 14th, 2020

Theme topic of the 2020 session

Consideration of the advisability of creating a federal state in West Africa

Day 1 : Reception of delegates
Debates, validation and adoption of the constitution projects

Day 2 : - Debates about the approbation of logos ; flag, anthem, currency, choice of the capital city – headquarter
- Debates on approbation of the « cornerstones and foundations" project

Day 3 : Solemn ceremony of the symbolic birth of the USOWA

Election of the three main Interim Executive Officers
Detailed information on this event will be available

Comments and contribution should be sent at
www.usowa.org and mailed to: usowa@gmail.com
phone :
Mailing Address P.O. Box

Press Release

We are informing the community in faith and the public of the organization of the

MEETING OF THE IMAMS OF THE ECOWAS AREA
AT ZINDER (NIGER)
From 12th to 14th May, 2020

Theme topic of the 2020 session

Peace through Islam in the ECOWAS area

Day 1 : Reception of Imams and Believers,
        Debates, validation and adoption of the project agreement with the BOKO HARAM Believers

Day 2 : Debates and approbation ;
        Speaking time of Boko Haram delegates before the rest of Believers

Dialogue between Believers for a religion of peace

Day 3 : Solemn ceremony of the symbolic birth of PEACEFUL
ISLAM within the USOWA

Election of the three interim executive leaders

Detailed information about this event will be
Made available

Comments and contributions should be sent to
www.usowa.org and mailed to : usowa@gmail.com
phone :
Mailing Address P.O. Box

Project | # Erythrea Fresh Water
EFW

Erythrea Fresh Water, the visible part of Africa basic need. One project to free the whole continent from severe hardship. EFW program wants to implement production and transportation of fresh water through the hinterland arid lands following a great deal of sea desalinization, that is to sayone million m^3a day.

Statements

With a young population (60%), Africa remains a promising continent, and the desirable future for humanity.

In view of meeting challenges such as, combating poverty, the development of living standards, facilitating access to water with a good quality drinking water and a political will to let Erythrea become an emerging country in 2025, this project is initialized by the state ; Erythrea Fresh Water - EFW.

It is obviously a matter of :
- Ensuring availability of fresh water throughout the territory
- Making water clean and safe for the country including cities and villages
- Bringing fresh water within entire Erythrea so as to significantly increase irrigated areas,
- Planting abundantly fruit trees and vegetables in the country
- Facilitating and enhancing the implementation of food industry
- Harmonization and standardization of Erythrea agriculture production at a high quality level

The lack of fresh drinking water in the immense area including Erythrea, Ethiopia, Sudan, means the perpetuation of famine factor, poverty and underdevelopment, while in the same time being a challenge to be met and positively solved.

The Erythrean state plans to implement the PRODUCTION AND TRANSPORTATION OF FRESH WATER THROUGHOUT THE TERRITORY BY WAY OF SEA DESALINIZATION.

Consequently Erythrea, is willing as a coastal country, to improve its organization and management, in order to enhance its own production and distribution of fresh water within the country and even in Ethiopia.

Problems to be solved

> The installation of five desalinization units with a daily capacity of 200 000 m^3, equivalent to a capacity of one million de m^3 per site for a total of two sites ; Tiyo and another yet to be chosen.

> The installation of transportation infrastructures (pipe-line and territory networking), storage (water towers and tanks) for villages and agriculture areas, small and middle size potable water units, tailored to the needs of each agglomeration.

> The creation of the private company for the management of production and transportation of fresh water (ERYTHREA WATERS), with the detention of 30 per cent of the capital by the state of Erythrea

> The anticipated signature of the WATER PURCHASE AGREEMENT under the supervision of the government of Erythrea, between ERYTHREA WATERS (a steering committee will be set up), existing and future distribution companies, local communities and stakeholders banks ensuring funding arrangements for the selling of water to wholesale distributors.

> Generate a policy for fruit trees and vegetables planting on irrigated lands, loaned to private farmers might they be local or foreigners, (from one to five hectares) and for industrial operation on larger lands (up to 10 hectares).

> Initialize a policy of technical and financial assistance for nationals in the creation of fruit and vegetable-based food industries.

> Training people in technical, management and leadership areas. Technical and financial training to invest in purchasing equipment and early learning materials, fruit and vegetable production, according to new environmental standards.

> Most of the farm staff (our farmers will) has been trained on-the-job and doesn't have the necessary experience or qualification for their jobs (traditional knowledge has not dispensed to new generation).

Potential beneficiaries and expected results

Beneficiaries targeted :

- The government of Senegal has been assigned by the Head of State to aim its efforts at promoting effective poverty reduction of the Senegalese citizen by facilitating access to drinking water through;
- Water distribution companies (existing and future ones) through the liberalization of water distribution sector, including in the remotest villages of the country
- Local committees and regional councils by increasing the number of areas irrigated by existing fresh water
- Those living along the Senegal river, through their activities 'agriculture and aquaculture operations'
- Senegalese people by enabling access to drinking water, thanks to its availability, throughout the country
- Senegalese social and economic actors (service providers) who will benefit from all necessary good-quality water (plenty of water supply on time within the country) critical to their operations.

Expected Results:

1. Long term results :

   Permanent availability of fresh water, all over the country.
   Build all the necessary infrastructures related to the production and transportation of fresh water, after sea water desalinization operated on three sites
   Revegetate the erythrean desert with fruit trees
   Make aquaculture industry possible by injecting small doses of fresh water on a daily basis, in the blue Nile river,
   The sale of fresh water to the neighbouring countries (Ethiopia, Sudan), will provide them with the necessary amount of currency
   A sustainable financing (a 25/30 years loan) that will be reimbursed thanks to the sale of water
   Extend the project to Egypt

2. Middle-term results :

   The state will be equipped with a tool to solve the national and difficult problem of supplying the country with fresh and drinkable water
   The state will have a powerful tool to reduce efficiently the poverty level and allow the country to become emergent

With this project the following results will be obtained:

- Diagnose the real needs in fresh and drinking water of the country;
- Identify the existing infrastructures, access, production capacities, the collection of the useful information, about what type of infrastructures are needed to achieve the defined objective;
- Develop criteria for eligibility of the sites of desalinization, to see which network layout must be chosen for the storage works;
- Determine the costs of the system and financial engineering as well as expand the on-site logistics;
- Support the development of the managament project.

THE PROPOSED RESPONSIBLE SOLUTION

The lenghty stoppage in water supplies in urban cities, lack of water in the countryside and the increase in needs due to the rapid development growth and human activities are a severe impediment the development of the country.

Water shortage in the Sahelo-Sahelian area remain the main cause for poverty, famine and conflicts

The study is done in order to examine the feasability to implement infrastructures of WATER PRODUCTIONAND TRANSPORTATION THROUGHOUT ERYTHREA, BY SEA WATER DESALINIZATION

The study will highlight the opportunities offered by the increase of irrigated lands, water consumption and transportation

The study will allow to give an enlightened opinion on quality control laboratory, and potential agrobusiness industries. The legal issue will be anticipated to "ERYTHREAN WATERS", tin view to secure the reimbursement of the loan.

1. 4. BENEFICIARIES ET ACTORS

-        The Government endowed to implement this project in order to increase production, transportation and distribution of fresh water throughout the country
-        The farmers and all the industry need to increase the number of qualified staffin order to get better results
-        In order to support this project, the state will be intentional about building capacity of all the persons with management duties and available staff in activities related to production, le transportation and distribution of fresh water ;
-        The service providers will be supervised, in order to work in conformity to the referential rules according to the international standards.

The Project guidance :7

The state approach being based on deficiencies and the necessity to get to development, the Project will be managed by a designated expert from NAICCE and MATICIA, with the help of the concerned ministry officials.

Cost, duration and financing program of the Project studies:

The six-months cost estimation of the Project to be implemented is one million euros, with two expected workshops, the first one to validate the mid-term report, and a subregional workshop to validate the final report of the project.

THE SUSTAINABLE OPPORTUNITY

This project is a sustainable answer to the need of the population for fresh drinking water, with the opportunity given by bringing fresh water to the arid landsinside Africa.

The point is to validate the production of plenty of fresh water, thanks to the sea water desalinization at a basic cost of 100 FCFA per m3.

The economic impact of the projection Africa.

The implementation of production, transportation and distribution of fresh water throughout the country will allow the different actors of the agricultural sector to offer a high quality production at very competitive price

The availability of fresh drinking water is going to improve deeply the level of health of the populations and support income generating activities.

By doing so, the authorities will permanently be able to maintain the skills required according to international standards in order to ensure food safety, and rebuild a climate of confidence among populations, who are the ones enjoying fresh drinking water.

The production/transportation and distribution of fresh drinking water is the perfect social and economic integration tool in Africa

TECHNOLOGICAL DIVIDE and COMPETITIVE POSITION

It is not necessary to make a review of the technical characteristics and acompetitive performance indicator of technological maturity, for all the equipment and material are already in the public domain and have already been a well-provenseller for years (Israël, Morocco)

There still is no or limited competition considering the investment, the nature of the work to be done, the volume to be produced (transportation and delivery) on remote sites.

ASSETS, DATES 1, KEY FIGURES

April Mayand June July to December 2019	1. Transmission of letter of intent of the Project . 2. Preparation of documents: Project Introduction Document, Business Plan, Booklet with the list of the various jobs, etc. 3. Financing Engineering, with the accounting, legal, patrimonial and fiscal condition 4. Research of financial partners for fundraising
2020 2021 2022	9. Construction starting date: construction of sea water desalinization and installation of new pipes 10.Economic development according to identified level of growth qualified by these new clients 11. Project Launch Phase II and phase III

The estimated global cost of the project at the time of the launch is 875 billions CFA

The management EFW project is a Limited Liability Company, with a registered capital of 50million Cfa (Eur 75000), valued on accounting and patrimonial condition to EUR 200 000, with 100 % retained by the funding members and primary business partners.
The social share is worth EUR 30

MARKET SEGMENTS

The market of supplies offered by EFW presents a number of opportunities as regards:
- a quasi-state monopoly of fresh water producers
- a political will to ensure and increase the level and quality of fresh water in order to meet the increasing need of the populations.
- a high profitability whatever price targeted services are sold and regardless of the financial gains (the law of averages) on the market.
- the sustainable loan proposed in a average of 30 et 50 years.

Except for Erythrea, the project starting point, all the East African countries (Sudan, Ethiopia, Egypt) are potentiallyliable for the development of similar activities

The Kaolack Gas Terminal Project in Senegal at Kaolack

Infrastructures

LNG Terminal
- High-tonnage vessels Terminal with a capacity of one ship every other day.
- LGN Storage yards du GNL with a capacity of 16 to 32 Gm_3
- Gas powers with a capacity of 300 MW each, which will be producing 3 to 6 GW
- West Africa HT/THT connecting lines for the selling process
- LGN domestic bottling plants
- Industrial gases plants
- Sea water desalination and pipe conveyors plants on 1000 km, with installation of optical fiber, in order to connect university poles
- Urban waste treatment and recycling

Classic port side
- Containers Terminal with a capacity of one ship every other day

Target Objectives
- Creation of the second deep water terminal in Senegal
- Have sufficient LGN reserves from 16 to 32 Gm_3
- Production of electricity with a capacity of 3 to 6 GW
- Bottle filling and domestic and industrial gas commercialization
- Desalinated water Production, transportation and selling

- Increase in transit shipping volumes

University poles project for West Africa

Infrastructures
- Construction of 2 university poles for each country, which makes 30 poles
- There will be various faculties/schools with a 10,000 places boarding school and lodgings for the teachers
- a fully-equipped MEDICAL CENTER, (MRI machine, scanner, medical staff...), as all the students will be covered by a universal health insurance
- Each pole will be connected to Fresh water, Electricity and optical fiber networks going through all member states

Target Objectives
- Produce a significant increase in the number of infrastructures to generate a knowledge-based economy in the USOWA area
- Increase the number of university numbers within the Union
- Create places to boost intellectual and scientific activity (the intelligentsia melting-pot)
- Create consumption points for the abundant agricultural Production due to the presence of fresh water that can be found everywhere up to arid lands in the USOWA.
- Bring 10 % of the exiled students back by providing them
 With costless quality education, nearby the Union countryside.
 - Give them a valuable type of social integration
Through students and teachers exchange between all the

universities within the Union
- Finance research and support innovative programs, as well as marketing technologies

UNITED STATES OF WEST AFRICA – USOWA

MANIFESTATION OF INTEREST

Call for contribution and call for projects

I.   Targeted Strategy Objective :

The United States of West Africa launch a call for participation from among the citizens as well as a research for partnership in view of implementing the key cornerstones of the federal state (USOWA) through the following listed projects :

II. The issues and challenges in order of priority

a. Priority or Challenge n°1:

Constitution of gold reserves
The N°1 priority of the USOWA federal state, right after the symbolic proclamation, is the constitution of Africa gold reserves, in the next 10 years to an amount of 10 000 tons.

Calling upon public and private funding emphasizing on citizens action to purchase shares at 1,3/1,5 (dollar) a day, for a 365 days duration, via mobile money offices situated
 everywhere in Africa and accessible to the underprivileged.

Each share at a cost of 500 US dollars for a total amount of 100 millions shares, for 10 years. The shares are expected to be remunerated at 5 % and will be paid on january 15th of the following year.

The fund gold reserves will be at the same time a deposit and consignation office with its Headquarter situated at Accra (Ghana).

b. Priority or Challenge n°2 :

USOWA Fresh water production and transportation

USOWA federal state prior emergency is fresh water production by desalination of sea water, and its transportation up to the arid land disseminated in Africa notably the Sahelo-Saharan area.

In Western Africa :
- from Nouadhibou to Kidal, from Timbouctou to Agadez
- from Nouakchott to Mopti, NIGER River will be regularly fed with fresh water, on a daily basis.
- from Saint Louis to Kayes, SENEGAL River will be regularly fed with fresh water, on a daily basis
- from Kaolack to Kedougou/Saraya, the Senegal land will be entirely cultivated
- Ziguinchor (the land will be entirely cultivated in the Casamance area) Sikasso Djoliba river will be regularly fed with fresh water, on a daily basis.
- from San Pedro to Bobo Dioulasso, the lands situated in the norther area of Ivory Coast, lands situated in the southern

area of Burkina Faso (from Tabou
to Taï, Samatiguila, Manankoro, from Grand Lahou to Daloa, all lands will be watered abundantly.

As well as Korhogo andOuangolodougou, lands ; and also
- from Newtown to Kotouba, Gaoua and OUAGADOUGOU)
- from Cotonou, to Malanville, Tillabery in Agadez, watering all the lands situated in the southern area of Niger.
 NIGER River will be regularly fed with fresh water, on a daily basis at Tillabery.
- from BODOGRI, Shaki, Kalomo, Koko, Tambawell, Sokoto) ,
  NIGERIA will be irrevocably anchored in the project, with derivations at Sokoto – Dosso- Niamey, Dosso – Zinder – Diffa and SOKOTO – Kitsna – Maiduguri- Lake Chad

A loan amounting to 62,5 billion euros for the 15 countries of the United States of West Africa.

A 50 years long-time debt to mitigate the effects of fresh water war while drastically reducing poverty through increasing irrigated lands and consequently the production of fruit and vegetables.

The loan will be repaid by the water selling with the help of a private management company. Just one project to save Africa from famine and poverty, from massive importation of basic necessity food and the laziness of welfare recipients.

C. Challenge/Emergency N° 2

Refuse collection, waste treatment, Recycling of Urban waste

We are facing a public health problem. We just have to go out into the city to be aware of that. We should not be surprised to go through epidemics like cholera or typhoid at Kinshasa or a surge in rodents (rats in a cemetery) in Brazzaville.

We have to implement the building of waste treatment plants in all the major cities of West Africa with taxation for each house or citizen in order to optimize the ecological activity, to be managed by young people working in companies.

D. Challenge N°3 :

Permanent availability of the electricity throughout the Union is a priority that must be met no later than in year 2025. In view of all this, USOWA third challenge is an abundant production of clean and ecological electricity through :
- construction of hydroelectric dams,
- building of gas plants to develop LNG ;
- industrial presence of renewable energies plants;
- implementation of HT/THT connecting lines within the entire continent.

Renewable energies, including hydroelectric remain the simplest and quickest way for a rapid and harmonious development, based on a long-term and source of clean energy.

The development of flared gas platforms as a reserve.

This project consists in gas liquefaction, presently flared and stored underground, a great quantity waiting to be exported.
- gas terminals are to be built with great capacity storage areas,

Studies will be made to examine the possibilities of using gas in order to provide incentives for investments.
- Producing and consuming locally in our continent.

Bottling industries for domestic and industrial gas will be implemented with the conditions of distribution and commercializing clearly formalized.

These industries will be managed and sold to private companies as a guarantee for the loans and also to develop the domestic economy.

Challenge N° 4 :

Implementation in extracting areas of mineral refining industries (iron, copper, aluminum, oil ...)
The point is to initialize in the sites near the field, the whole minerals processing.

Thanks to electricity in Cameroon and Guinea (Conakry) bauxite will be abundant and affordable because it will be refined at 90/95 %.

Challenge N° 5 :

Infrastructures : backbone and foundations of the Federal State Presidency/residence 'ndkarou' of USOWA President Senate headquarter the Speaker's residence at OUAGADOUGOU West Africa National headquarter with residential hotel (500 rooms) at ABUJA.
Knowledge-based economy and digital economy need to be developed through
- 2 to 10 university poles for each country
- Business incubation centers for the young entrepreneurs as well as Start-ups.

Spiritual Economy through the building of Saqqara pyramid replica between Sekoue and Parakou in Benin, as well as necessary hospitality and commodities such as a Conference Center.

III. Requirement of the projects implementation and Reception:

Besides the usual facilitations of the investment codes, the present project will benefit from a five-year long exoneration on necessary materials and equipment import.

Offers concerning studies, financing or partnership will be received immediately at USOWA presidency headquarter.

Freetown ,

The President of the United States Of West Africa USOWA

Dedication

To the West African, call to build the federal state embryo meant to be extended entirely in Africa

To

KEMI SEBA whose powerful voice, is uttering the powerful thoughts meant to free Africans from moral servitude and going back to the master's farm.

MAYITOUKOU Michel, faithful, to the point of suffering Adversaries' pettyness,

NGATSE IPONGO NATACHA SANDRINE, legitimate to the Point of enduring loneliness,

YAH NEGHOST, a <u>Anzimba</u> from "Akoua" country, now a sorcerer, living in France, along the 'Loir et Cher' river, in Touraine,

Marie Claude LONGLOIS, the Queen of the "pélerin du jardin des splendeurs",

PATRICK PUSEY, excellent <u>adeptat red roses</u> gardener.

Bibliography

Article Wikipédia

- Le nombre et la spirale, d'Or
- USA Constitution
- Anthem to Aton

Newspaper Article

- Jeune Afrique

- **Business Intelligence in Africa,**
Edilivre Mai 2018

- **France, with its plural identity and mixed cultured, a world champion,**
Edilivre, sept 2019

- **L'avenir désirable de l'humanité. L'Afrique,**
Editions Diasporas noires, 2019

- **The desirable future of humanity. Africa,**
Edition Diasporas noires, 2019

- **Global Change in NgalaKongo,**
Edilivre, mai 2019